The BIG Marathon

The runners are lining up for the start of today's race.
Be part of the action! Find and color:

❑baseball cap ❑bunny slippers ❑clown ❑blimp ❑f…
❑flat tire ❑flying saucer ❑kangaroo ❑lost hig…
❑mailbox ❑parking meter ❑skateboard ❑t…

Mall Madness

It's a rainy Saturday afternoon and this shopping mall
is jumping! Find and color:

❏ballerina ❏balloon ❏bass drum ❏bicycle ❏❏❏❏❏❏birds [6] ❏clown ❏donkey
❏doughnut ❏fire hydrant ❏flying saucer ❏football helmet ❏four-leaf clover
❏giant apple ❏giant pretzel ❏giant jack-o-lantern ❏owl ❏parachute
❏picnic basket ❏giant pie ❏plunger ❏teddy bear ❏toy car
❏tree ❏umbrella ❏wagon

Holiday Land

Here's a place where everyone's favorite holiday characters
go to relax. Find and color:

❑balloon ❑broom ❑candy cane ❑❑elephants [2] ❑four-leaf clover ❑heart
❑rocking horse ❑hot air balloon ❑kangaroo ❑lamb ❑lost sock
❑mermaid ❑mouse ❑noisemaker ❑old-fashioned radio ❑pear tree
❑piggy bank ❑pilgrim hat ❑rowboat ❑teapot ❑tepee ❑turtle
❑umbrella ❑vest ❑wheelbarrow ❑yo-yo

Airport Antics
It's just another typical day at this busy international airport . . . or is it?
Find and color:

❑apple ❑beret ❑cactus ❑❑clowns [2] ❑crayon ❑flower
❑license plate ❑gorilla ❑megaphone ❑mouse ❑necktie ❑paintbrush
❑palm tree ❑periscope ❑pig ❑saxophone ❑sea horse ❑shark fin
❑sunglasses ❑surfboard ❑tin man ❑unicycle
❑woolen cap ❑yo-yo ❑zebra

Happy Birthday!

There's fun to spare at this action-packed birthday party. Find and color:

❑artist's paintbrush ❑birdhouse ❑birthday girl ❑bugle ❑beach ball
❑cowboy hat ❑dog ❑frog ❑genie's lamp ❑globe ❑jack-in-the-box
❑mitten ❑polka-dotted bow ❑pumpkin ❑rocking chair ❑scarf
❑shorts ❑straw hat ❑sunglasses ❑top hat ❑toy race car
❑woolen cap ❑❑❑❑❑❑❑wrapped gifts [8]

The Comic Book Store

If you like comic books, there's nothing that you can't find here—including your favorite superhero! Find and color:

❑apple ❑bell ❑❑❑❑❑eyeglasses [5] ❑fire hydrant ❑flippers ❑flowerpot
❑flying bat ❑flying saucer ❑football helmet ❑Glove-Man ❑guitar
❑ice skates ❑lightning bolt ❑musical notes ❑oil can ❑palm tree
❑scarecrow ❑shovel ❑slippers ❑snake ❑sombrero
❑super-duper teddy bear ❑top hat ❑volcano

Home Improvement

Family and friends are busy fixing up the Wilsons' house. Maybe they are making *too* many improvements at once! Find and color:

❏ax ❏barrel ❏❏❏❏baseball caps [4] ❏book ❏carrot ❏ceiling fan
❏fish ❏football ❏gopher ❏ice cream cone ❏key ❏kite ❏lamp ❏lizard
❏moose head ❏palm tree ❏party hat ❏pear ❏pumpkin ❏skateboard
❏toothbrush ❏top hat ❏toy locomotive ❏trumpet ❏watering can

Is the Doctor In Today?

There is no shortage of patients (and patience) at this busy doctor's office.
Find and color:

☐balloon ☐binoculars ☐closed umbrella ☐coffee mug ☐crown
☐digital clock ☐duck ☐fire hydrant ☐gecko ☐graduation cap
☐heart ☐high-top sneakers ☐ice cream cone ☐jester's cap
☐lampshade ☐oil can ☐overalls ☐pay phone ☐propeller beanie cap
☐skeleton key ☐star ☐teddy bear ☐tv ☐untied necktie ☐vase

Miniature Golf

Prepare to have maximum fun on this miniature golf course. Find and color:

❏alligator ❏garden hose ❏giant flower ❏giant ice cream cone ❏giant teacup
❏horse ❏kite ❏life preserver ❏mailbox ❏necktie ❏old tire ❏palm tree
❏pirate flag ❏pogo stick ❏rocket ship ❏shark fin ❏shovel ❏snake
❏stop sign ❏tombstone ❏toy truck ❏traffic light
❏umbrella ❏windmill ❏wrapped gift

Moving the Mail

No matter the weather, these postal employees get letters and packages to their destinations. Find and color:

❑accordion ❑arrow ❑banana peel ❑barbell ❑basketball ❑bowling ball ❑bow tie ❑broom ❑chimney ❑ear of corn ❑flagpole ❑flat tire ❑frying pan ❑ladder ❑mailbox ❑mitten ❑paper airplane ❑party hat ❑scarf ❑telescope ❑top hat ❑turtle ❑vacuum cleaner ❑welcome mat ❑wind-up toy car

Backyard Gardeners

Does this hard-working group have what it takes to grow
a beautiful garden? Find and color:

❑backpack ❑backwards baseball cap ❑BIG clown shoes ❑bunny slippers
❑butterfly ❑cowboy hat ❑crocodile ❑dustpan ❑football ❑frog ❑gloves
❑heart ❑hedge clippers ❑jump rope ❑kite ❑mermaid ❑pumpkin
❑shovel ❑snake ❑spinning top ❑toolbox ❑watering can
❑wedge of cheese ❑wheelbarrow ❑wrapped gift

Career Day

What do you want to be when you grow up? Find and color:

❑apple core ❑barrel ❑baseball cap ❑birdhouse ❑bouquet of flowers
❑bowl of oranges ❑broom ❑candy cane ❑dinosaur ❑drum ❑football
❑giant crayon ❑globe ❑heart ❑kite ❑lion ❑pear ❑pickax
❑pumpkin ❑sailboat ❑skateboard ❑top hat
❑toy locomotive ❑tree ❑watering can

Theme Park Fun

You have entered a *very* unusual theme park—take a look around. Find and color:

❏banana peel ❏blimp ❏bow tie ❏burst balloon ❏cactus ❏carrot
❏caveman ❏crown ❏doghouse ❏empty flowerpot ❏hard hat ❏hot-air balloon
❏kangaroo ❏lost sock ❏mermaid ❏mouse ❏palm tree ❏rocking chair
❏rocking horse ❏runaway balloon ❏Santa cap
❏seal ❏snow skis ❏welcome mat ❏wizard

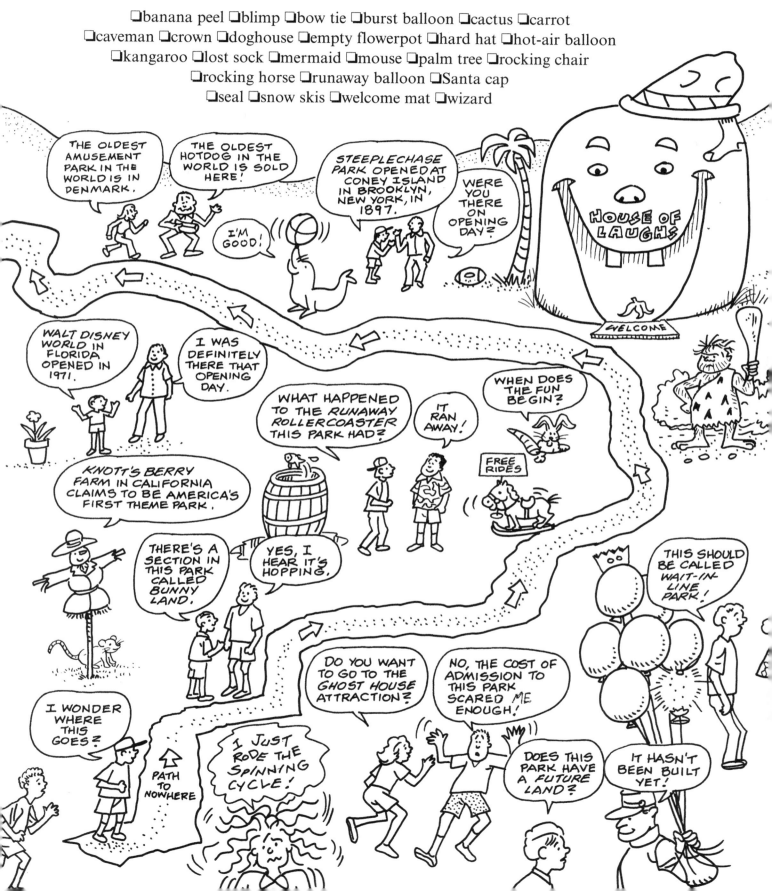

Play Ball!

It's opening day for the Galveston Gophers, a very minor league baseball team.
Find and color:

❑anchor ❑balloon ❑basketball ❑bowling ball ❑coffee mug ❑daisy
❑fish ❑goalie mask ❑golf bag ❑leprechaun ❑lost sock ❑mouse ears
❑mustache ❑oil can ❑pirate ❑propeller cap ❑pumpkin
❑REAL gopher ❑safari helmet ❑scarecrow ❑surfboard
❑teddy bear ❑trophy ❑walking cane ❑yo-yo

Opening Night

The curtain is about to go up on this new stage production. Will it come down after only one performance? Find and color:

❏alligator ❏beret ❏bird ❏butterfly ❏football helmet ❏four-leaf clover
❏guitar ❏horseshoe ❏ice cream cone ❏jack-in-the-box ❏jester's cap
❏ladder ❏lost mitten ❏lost sock ❏mermaid ❏mushroom ❏necktie
❏owl ❏plunger ❏rose ❏scarf ❏suspenders
❏tepee ❏ten-gallon hat ❏tin man

Playground Fun for All
It's great to be a kid . . . isn't it? Find and color:

❑apple core ❑arrow ❑backpack ❑backwards baseball cap ❑bear
❑bicycle horn ❑cactus ❑cowboy hat ❑football ❑four-leaf clover
❑graduation cap ❑hula hoop ❑lamppost ❑license plate ❑lost sock
❑musical note ❑owl ❑paper clip ❑pencil ❑Santa cap ❑suspenders
❑traffic cone ❑trash can ❑turtle ❑untied necktie

Freshly Baked Goods

What are those wonderful smells coming from this popular bakery?
Let's find out! Find and color:

❑bandana ❑baseball cap ❑broom ❑candy cane ❑crown ❑frog
❑heart ❑hot dog ❑key ❑lock ❑old-fashioned radio ❑paintbrush
❑piggy bank ❑pinwheel ❑pogo stick ❑rocket ship ❑roller skates
❑sailboat ❑snake ❑straw hat ❑sunglasses ❑teapot
❑toothbrush ❑vest ❑watering can

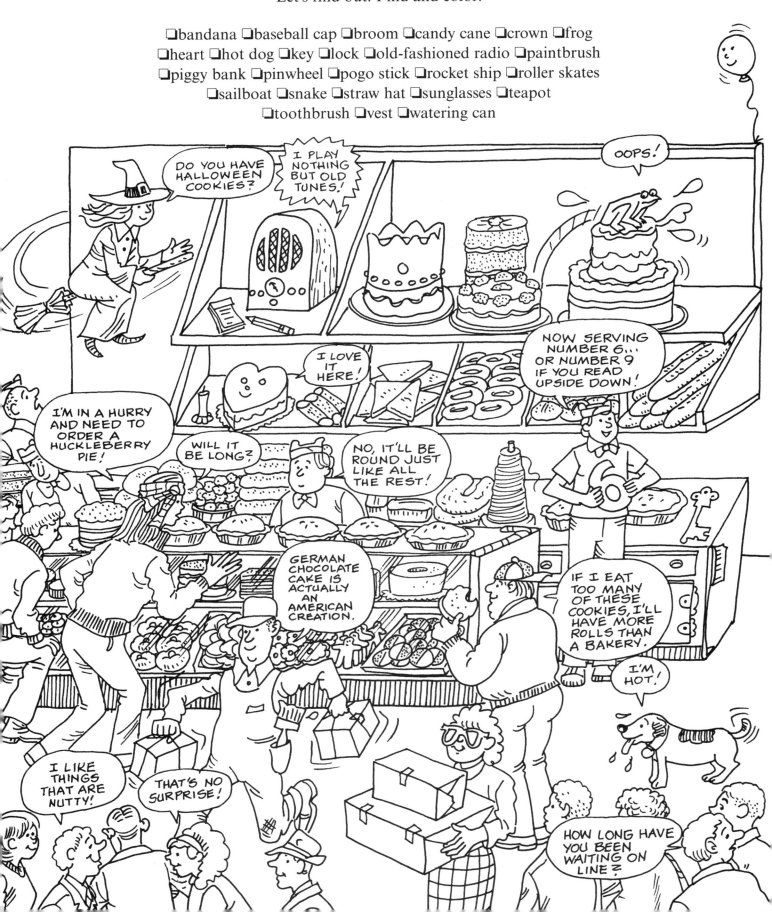

Trick or Treat!

It's October 31, and little ghosts and goblins and other costumed creatures are searching for sweets. Find and color:

❑anchor ❑ax ❑balloon ❑banana peel ❑broom ❑clown ❑flower
❑lamppost ❑mitten ❑penguin ❑periscope ❑pioneer ❑pirate
❑❑pumpkins [2] ❑robot ❑skunk ❑sombrero ❑star ❑stop sign
❑teddy bear ❑traffic light ❑umbrella ❑Uncle Sam
❑watermelon slice ❑wheelbarrow

Your Public Library

A library is a quiet place to read and learn. So what happened
to this library? Find and color:

❑apple ❑balloon ❑bow tie ❑cactus ❑carrot ❑crown ❑drum
❑fire hydrant ❑flower ❑flying bat ❑football ❑giant pencil ❑globe
❑hammer ❑kite ❑mouse ❑oar ❑pumpkin ❑Santa cap ❑star
❑surfboard ❑top hat ❑tuba ❑turtle ❑umbrella

Our Nation's Forefathers

What if some of the most famous Americans made a surprise visit to your classroom? Find and color:

❏arrow ❏baseball glove ❏bell ❏bugle ❏raccoon skin cap ❏cupcake
❏daisy ❏dunce cap ❏fish ❏flowerpot ❏headband ❏hockey stick
❏jack-o-lantern ❏life preserver ❏lollipop ❏lost sneaker ❏musical note
❏palm tree ❏picture frame ❏rocking chair ❏snake ❏spray can
❏straw basket ❏toy truck ❏wastepaper basket

In the Days of Dinosaurs

What if dinosaurs weren't as "prehistoric" as we think? Find and color:

❑birdhouse ❑cactus ❑drum ❑flying bat ❑flying saucer ❑garbage can
❑gavel ❑genie's lamp ❑graduation cap ❑hatchet ❑hockey stick
❑knight in armor ❑oar ❑owl ❑palm tree ❑periscope
❑plunger ❑Santa cap ❑scarf ❑shovel ❑spray can
❑stop sign ❑teapot ❑traffic cone ❑windmill

In the Swim

It's fun to go swimming in a community pool on a hot summer day!
Find and color:

❏apple ❏backwards baseball cap ❏balloon ❏beach ball
❏butterfly ❏candy cane ❏drum ❏duck ❏easel ❏fish ❏giant crayon
❏❏heart [2] ❏kite ❏lion ❏mermaid ❏mouse ❏oar
❏periscope ❏sea horse ❏suitcase ❏tin man
❏toy truck ❏umbrella ❏whistle

Technology Rules!

Have gadgets like computers made our lives easier or more complicated?
You decide! Find and color:

❏baby rattle ❏ball of yarn ❏beach ball ❏elephant
❏guitar ❏headphones ❏lamp ❏pencil ❏piggy bank
❏plant ❏purse ❏REAL mouse ❏stool